ENCYCLOPEDIA OF NEW YEAR'S CELEBRATIONS AROUND THE WORLD

Melissa Crawford

CONTENTS

Rigby

A Harcourt Achieve Imprint

www.Rigby.com

1-800-531-5015

Introduction

Throughout the world, countries celebrate the beginning of a new year in different ways. Some countries have been celebrating this holiday for hundreds, even thousands of years, while other celebrations are relatively new.

The flooding of the Nile marked the beginning of the new year for people in ancient Egypt.

Our world is rich in traditions and full of interesting people, places, and celebrations. In the United States, you might celebrate New Year's Eve at a party with friends, whereas in other parts of the world, you might celebrate by gathering with family to look at the moon.

In this encyclopedia, you will visit all of the continents of the world and you will explore several **cultural** groups. As you examine the history and traditions behind New Year festivals, you will gain a better understanding of the groups and their cultures. Likewise, you will begin to see similarities among cultures you once thought were very different from one another.

People in many countries celebrate the new year with fireworks.

New Year's Celebrations Around the World

We'll be exploring celebrations in twenty places.

Africa
1. Northern Africa (Egypt, Morocco, Tunisia)
2. Swaziland
3. South Africa

Antarctica
4. South Pole

Asia
5. China
6. India
7. Israel
8. Japan
9. Korea
10. Thailand
11. Vietnam

Europe
12. Germany
13. Russia
14. Scotland
15. Spain

North America
16. United States

Oceania
17. Australia
18. New Zealand

South America
19. Argentina
20. Brazil

NORTH AMERICA
16

ATLANTIC

SOUTH AMERICA
20

PACIFIC OCEAN

19

4

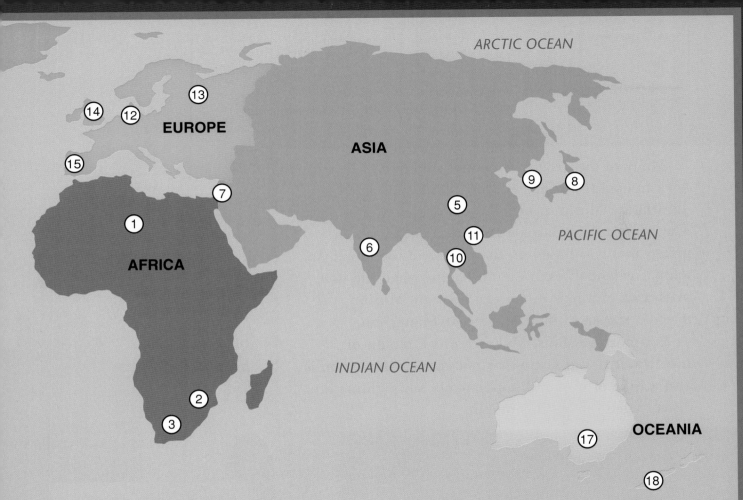

ARCTIC OCEAN

EUROPE

ASIA

AFRICA

PACIFIC OCEAN

INDIAN OCEAN

OCEANIA

SOUTHERN OCEAN

ANTARCTICA ④

5

Africa

Many of the groups of people who live in North African countries such as Morocco, Egypt, and Tunisia are Muslims, or followers of the religion Islam. The Islamic calendar is a **lunar** calendar, which means that it is based on the phases of the moon. In a lunar calendar, each month begins when the first **crescent** of a new moon can be seen. Muslims call the first month of their lunar year Muharram.

For most Muslims, Muharram is a month of **meditation** and fasting, or not eating. Muharram is also a time of peace; disagreements and fighting are discouraged during this month.

Many Muslims celebrate Muharram in meditation at mosques like this one.

The first day of Muharram is the start of the Islamic New Year. Not all Muslims celebrate this day, but those who do celebrate it in many different ways. Some spend the day in quiet thought, while others give gifts and cards to friends and family.

Because the Islamic calendar year is 11 to 12 days shorter than a **solar** year, or a year based on the movements of the sun, Muharram changes dates every year. For example, the first day of Muharram, and the first day of the Islamic New Year, 2008, will be January 10. The last day of the first month of that year will be February 8, 2008.

Some people in Egypt celebrate the beginning of the New Year with fireworks.

Incwala is an old cultural tradition in Swaziland, a small country in Southern Africa. It lasts for several days between December and January. The timing of the celebration depends on the first full moon of the winter **solstice**. The word *Incwala* means "Festival of the First Fruits."

The Swazi people wear traditional costumes during Incwala.

Incwala has two parts: Little Incwala and Big Incwala. Little Incwala begins two days before the full moon after the winter solstice. During this time, people dress in traditional Swazi outfits and sing songs.

On the first day of Big Incwala, men walk more than twenty-five miles to get branches from a bush called lusekwane. For the next two days, the people wear traditional outfits and chant while the king hides in a hut. On the third day, the people dance around the king's hut and ask him to come out. When he finally does, he dances and eats the first pumpkin of the new harvest. His eating of the pumpkin lets the people know that their ancestors have blessed the harvest, and it is safe to eat.

After a day of rest and meditation, the people build a huge bonfire to burn things that represent the past year, including household items. The Swazi people ask their ancestors to bring rain to put out the fire, and then they hold feasts with much singing and dancing.

Pumpkins are important to the economy of Swaziland.

Cape Town is a small city in South Africa. It makes up for its small size with the number of festivals it holds each year. The largest of these is a carnival that begins on New Year's Day and continues well into January.

During the carnival there is much singing, dancing, and parading through the streets. The singers and dancers borrow from a variety of traditions to spice up the parades and music. Most of the songs performed are folk songs, but songs from North America and popular Latin and hip-hop dance tunes are often heard in the mix. Costume competitions are also held at the end of the carnival each year.

In 1986, former South African President Nelson Mandela showed his support for the event by donating money to the group that plans and hosts the carnival. He is now a member of this group.

Many different clubs, or *klopse,* perform during the carnival.

SUMMER • • • IN WINTER!

Summer in Cape Town starts in November and lasts until February.

SOUTH POLE 24 HOURS TO CELEBRATE

Even though its name means "the opposite of the Arctic," Antarctica is the coldest, driest, and windiest continent—98 percent of it is covered in ice. Because there is little rain, the interior of the continent is also technically the largest desert in the world. Only certain plants and animals can survive there, including penguins, fur seals, mosses, lichens, and many types of algae.

Workers at the Scott Base celebrate the new year with workers from McMurdo Station.

If you lived at the South Pole in Antarctica, you could cheer in the new year 24 times! You could also walk all the way around the world in just a few seconds. That is because all 24 lines of **longitude** come together at the South Pole. Since the lines of longitude tell what time zone a place is in, the South Pole is also in all 24 world time zones!

No one who lives at the South Pole is a native of the area, however. The population is made up of the permanent and part-time staff who work at the research facilities run by 26 different countries.

Every year, people who work at McMurdo Station for the U. S. Antarctic Program hold a big New Year's party in one of their workshops. Bands play, and everyone eats and dances until well past midnight.

The South Pole has another yearly tradition that happens around the new year—the placement of a marker telling the exact location of the South Pole. This marker has to be changed every year because the ice moves at a rate of about 39 feet per year.

Population of South Pole in Summer and Winter

SUMMER

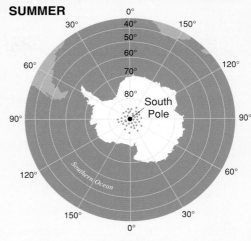

 = 100 people

WINTER

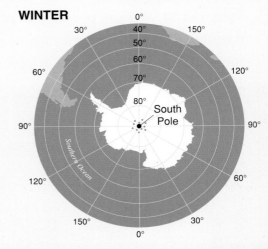

People have celebrated the Chinese New Year for so many years that the exact beginnings of the festival are not known. However, there are ancient customs that do have clear roots in Chinese culture. For example, on the actual first day of the new year (Chinese New Year lasts for fifteen days), an ancient custom called Hong Bao takes place. On this day, also known as Red Packet Day, adults put money in red envelopes and pass them out to younger people and children. Red is traditionaly seen as a lucky color, and money is a standard gift for important occasions.

Hong Bao packets come in many beautiful designs.

14

People start preparing for Chinese New Year one month before the first day. They buy decorations, clothing, food, and presents. They also clean their houses to sweep away bad luck, and sometimes paint the houses red. Families host traditional Chinese New Year's Eve dinners with a variety of foods. Most people wear red to this meal, as this color is believed to bring good luck.

The Chinese New Year celebration ends with the Festival of Lanterns, which always takes place under a full moon. This festival is believed to be 2,000 years old. No one knows its exact history, but there are many legends that explain its beginnings.

In one legend, the Jade Emperor was very angry at a town for eating his favorite goose. To teach them a lesson, he said he would destroy the town with a fire. A fairy heard of his plan and warned the people to light lanterns on the chosen day. They obeyed, and it looked like the village was on fire. Because of this, the Jade Emperor did not destroy the town.

Chinese Lion Dancers perform during the Festival of Lanterns.

15

In India, citizens celebrate the beginning of the year with a festival of lights called Diwali. Diwali begins on the first day of the Hindu calendar and lasts for five days. The Hindu culture is the main culture of India. Diwali always occurs in November, but the dates vary from year to year.

Lamps are lit during Diwali to represent hope.

There are many legends related to this festival but no certainty as to how it began. One popular legend involves King Dashratha, his three wives, and his four sons. One wife wanted her son, Bharat, to be the next king. However, the king wanted his son Rama to be his successor. The mother of Bharat made Rama leave for 14 years. Diwali is the festival that celebrates Rama's return home.

People celebrate Diwali by gathering fresh flowers, exchanging gifts, buying or making new clothes, and feasting with friends and family. Some people decorate their doorways during the holiday season and leave red and white footprints throughout their homes.

These flowers, made of colored sand, decorate the doorway of an Indian home during Diwali.

Most people in Israel and Jewish people around the world celebrate the Jewish New Year, or Rosh Hashanah. Yom Teruah and Yom Zikaron Teruah are other names for the holiday.

Rosh Hashanah lasts for 48 hours. This is really the first two days of the Jewish calendar, but the holiday is treated as if it were one long day. On this 48-hour day, a ram's horn called a *shofar* is sounded. This is the one of the few times during the year that this horn is blown.

The person who plays th
is called *Ba'al Tokea* whi
"Master of the Blast."

On the first day of Rosh Hashanah, Jewish people visit a body of water that contains fish. Using bread to represent the things they have done wrong over the year, they cast their wrongdoings into the water to be forgiven.

Dinner on the first night of Rosh Hashanah starts with apples dipped in honey. Jewish people also eat special bread called Challah, which is baked in a circle. This bread symbolizes the cycle of the year.

The period that begins with Rosh Hashanah ends ten days later on Yom Kippur. On Yom Kippur, Jewish people ask forgiveness for things they have done wrong during the year.

Jewish men gather at a lake to say a prayer on the first day of Rosh Hashanah.

BY THE SEA

Part of Israel's border is the Mediterranean Sea, also known as "the middle sea."

Mediterranean Sea

Israel

Shogatsu, held between the first and third of January, is the most important holiday in Japan. In fact, most businesses shut down between January 1 and January 3. People want to spend time with their families during the Japanese New Year.

It is a tradition in Japan to visit temples and **shrines** during Shogatsu. Over one million people visit the Meiji Shrine in the three days that celebrate the Japanese New Year. At midnight of January 1, people also listen as the bells on Buddhist temples throughout the country are rung 108 times to bring in the new year.

The Meiji Shrine in Tokyo, Japan was built to honor Emperor Meiji and his wife, Empress Shoken.

One Japanese New Year tradition actually starts before January 1. People purchase and write New Year's postcards to send to family members, friends, and people they know through work. These cards are called *nengajo*. If someone has had a death in the family, that person sends out postcards telling others *not* to send them nengajo. The cards are delivered on New Year's Day.

These are traditonal Japanese nengajo cards.

New Year's Day itself is a quiet day; people usually stay home. The second and third days bring more activity, however, as people visit friends and go shopping. During the three days of the celebration, the Japanese eat different types of food, depending on the region. Families usually eat soup on New Year's Day, but other popular foods include black beans, fish eggs, and fish.

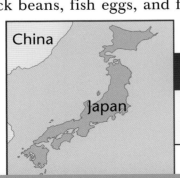

China

Japan

AN ISLAND NATION

Four main islands and several smaller islands make up Japan.

Koreans call their New Year's Day Sol-Nal. Sol-Nal lasts just for one day, although many people celebrate Sol-Nal twice: once on the first day of the calendar year and again on the first day of the lunar year, which is in February.

Jishin Balpgi, which means "Stepping on the Spirit of the Earth," is a festival in some parts of Korea. It marks the beginning of the lunar year. During this festival people chase away the bad luck of the old year by beating on drums and gongs. People also renew friendships, building a greater sense of community.

During the Jishin Balpgi festival, performers visit homes and wish people good fortune in the year to come. As a thank-you, residents offer the performers rice cakes. That evening, everyone gathers at the center of the village or town to enjoy the first full moon of the year together.

During Jishin Balpgi, people bang on drums to drive away bad luck.

23

Songkran, the Thai New Year, is celebrated from April 13 to April 15. It is also celebrated in Laos and Myanmar. A similar celebration called Sinhalese and Tamil New Year is held in Sri Lanka on the same dates. Because it is celebrated in so many countries, Songkran is also called the Southeast Asian New Year.

Songkran happens in the hottest part of the year in Thailand, at the end of the dry season. Perhaps because of this, people celebrate by throwing water on each other. They roam the streets with bowls of water and even garden hoses, splashing and spraying each other. This activity is rooted in tradition, however; pouring a small amount of water on someone's hands shows the person respect.

Buddhists bathe statues of the Buddha during Songkran.

Even though Songkran looks like a lot of fun, it has a serious side. The festival was started to teach important lessons, such as respect for the older generation. People visit older relatives and people in the community and bring them small gifts.

Songkran is also a time for cleaning and for changing one's behavior. People make promises to do more good things in the next year. They also clean their homes and clean statues and images of the Buddha, their spiritual leader. They also pile sand in the temples to make up for the sand they take away on their feet throughout the year.

People pile sand in Buddhist temples during Songkran.

The Vietnamese New Year's celebration lasts for seven days. This celebration is called Tet or Nguyendan, which means "the first morning of the first day of the new year."

On the thirtieth day of the twelfth month of the lunar calendar, Vietnamese people say goodbye to the old year. They then welcome the new year on midnight of that day. On the third day of the first month of the lunar calendar, the Vietnamese hold a ceremony in which they see the souls of their ancestors cross over into the next world.

Tet is often celebrated with beautiful lighted floats.

Agriculture, such as rice farming, is very important in Vietnam. Here, workers are harvesting the rice crop.

Tet is very important in Vietnam not only for its spiritual and religious values but also for its connection to **agriculture**. Tet occurs between the harvesting of crops and the planting of seeds for new crops.

The Vietnamese start preparing for this celebration many weeks before it actually occurs. This preparation includes cleaning homes to get rid of bad luck from the prior year. Some families pay their debts and resolve quarrels with friends, family, and neighbors. Others paint their homes inside and outside for a new look.

WHAT'S IN A NAME?

Names in Vietnam are different from those in the United States. Last names come first, then middle names, then first names.

GERMANY   SILVESTER

Germany, one of the largest countries in Europe, is often called "the land of thinkers." Many important writers, scientists, and philosophers have come from this nation. In addition, Berlin is often called the cultural capital of Europe. It is second only to Paris as a European tourist destination.

Fireworks explode over the dome of the Reichstag, a government building, on New Year's Eve in Berlin.

In Germany, New Year's Eve is called Silvester because December 31st is the feast day of Saint Silvester. Saint Silvester was a pope who lived in the fourth century. He was said to have been able to cure leprosy, a terrible disease that affects the skin.

Germans usually spend New Year's Eve with their friends, either celebrating quietly or at New Year's Eve parties, sometimes called "Silvester Balls." In cities such as Berlin, fireworks go off at midnight and people cheer the New Year.

People also play games meant to tell them what the year to come might have in store. One such activity is lead casting, in which people pour molten lead into a bowl of water and look for figures and meanings in the shapes into which the lead hardens. Often the lead figure is held up to a candle or other light and the shape of its shadow aids in this important decision.

Saint Silvester

Kits for *Bliegiessen*, or lead casting, can be bought at many German stores.

Russia, stretching across Europe and Asia, has the largest amount of land of any country in the world. Because of its size, it shares borders with fourteen other countries. It also has the world's eighth largest population.

Russians celebrate two New Year's Eves and Days. How can this be? Until 1918, Russia used a Julian calendar, which is different from our current Gregorian calendar by 10 to 13 days. In 1918, however, Russia's leader, Vladimir Lenin, switched to the Gregorian calendar. In doing so, he also gave the people of Russia two sets of holidays!

New Year's is a very important holiday for Russians. People see in the new year at midnight on December 31st with huge parties full of food, music and dancing. At midnight, everyone listens to chimes ringing 12 o'clock.

Russian holiday tradition includes a decorated fir tree, which is called a New Year's tree. Children look forward to a visit from Grandfather Frost who brings them presents. His granddaughter, Snowmaiden, also comes along to help him hand out the gifts.

But the celebration isn't over on January 2. At midnight on January 13, Russians gather again to celebrate Old New Year. This date is December 31 on the Julian calendar.

January

☐ Gregorian Calendar — New New Year's Day ☐ Julian Calendar — Old New Year's Day
✴ New New Year's Day ✴ Old New Year's Day

Sunday	Monday	Tuesday	Wednesday	Thursday	Friday	Saturday
		✴ 1 / December 19	2 / 20	3 / 21	4 / 22	5 / 23
6 / 24	7 / 25	8 / 26	9 / 27	10 / 28	11 / 29	12 / 30
13 / 31	14 / January 1 ✴	15 / 2	16 / 3	17 / 4	18 / 5	19 / 6
20 / 7	21 / 8	22 / 9	23 / 10	24 / 11	25 / 12	26 / 13
27 / 14	28 / 15	29 / 16	30 / 17	31 / 18		

RUSSIA'S TWO CALENDARS

Russia is not alone in following two calendars. Several other places, such as Jerusalem, Macedonia, Serbia, Georgia, and Ukraine, also celebrate certain holidays according to dates on the Julian calendar.

In Scotland, New Year's Day is called Hogmanay. It is an old holiday and more important to the Scots than any other holiday. During Hogmanay people burn fires to ward off bad luck.

There are many **rituals** and traditions associated with Hogmanay. One of these rituals is the Burning of the Clavie. The clavie is a barrel filled with wood shavings and tar which is lit on fire and rolled down a hill. Once it burns out, people gather some of the burning **embers** to bring back to their homes for good luck in the coming year.

Another tradition is "first footing." To bring good luck, the first guest to walk into a house on New Year's Day should be a tall man with dark hair. He should also be carrying gifts of food and coal.

In one town in Scotland, people walk the streets with baskets of fire. At the end of the parade, the baskets are thrown into the sea.

33

Noche Vieja, or Spanish New Year is focused on family. Celebrations usually takes place at home. However, thousands of people gather on New Year's Eve in Puerta del Sol Square in Madrid to hear the bell of the clock ring. As the clock strikes midnight, everyone eats twelve grapes, one on each ring of the bell. This is believed to bring good luck for the twelve months of the new year.

Thousands of people gather in Puerta del Sol Square in Madrid to hear the bell ring at midnight.

Eating grapes is a tradition that started when, after a particularly good grape harvest, the king of Spain gave everyone grapes to eat on New Year's Eve.

After midnight, it is common for people to go out to restaurants or friends' homes. The streets become overrun with music, streamers, and laughter.

AFTERNOON NAP

In Spain, many shops and offices close during the lunch hour. People go home to eat lunch and take a nap.

Grapes are very important to the economy of Spain.

UNITED STATES NEW YEAR'S EVE AND KWANZAA

People in the United States often celebrate New Year's Eve and New Year's Day with parties. On New Year's Eve, people make **resolutions** for the year to come and some even give gifts.

New Year's Eve parties are very common in the United States. Thousands of people gather each year at Times Square in New York City and in other public places. At midnight, bells ring, sirens sound, fireworks light up the sky, and everyone sings out, "Happy New Year!"

The Kwanzaa Karumu, or feast, is an African American tradition that is also usually held on December 31st. Families and whole communities take part in the feasts where everything is decorated red, black, and green. Traditional African music and dances are also performed.

New Year's Day is quieter than New Year's Eve. Family and friends sometimes spend it at home watching football games and parades on television. In the southern states, people eat black-eyed peas for good luck.

Some people also attend sporting events or parades, such as the Tournament of Roses Parade in Pasadena, California, or the Mummers' Parade in Philadelphia, Pennsylvania.

In many northern cities near bodies of water, people plunge into the cold water on New Year's Day. One of the oldest clubs hosting such an event is the Coney Island Polar Bears Club in New York. Members of this group have been taking an icy plunge in the Atlantic Ocean every year since 1903.

The Mummers' Parade is a tradition that was brought from England to the United States.

AUSTRALIA NEW YEAR'S EVE DOWN UNDER

Many people in Australian cities celebrate News Year's Eve with parties. With crowds of more than 1.2 million people, Sydney has the second largest New Year's Eve celebration worldwide. But unlike America's chilly eve, Australia's New Year's Eve is often a warm summer night. Because Australia is in the southern hemisphere, New Year's comes in the middle of that country's summer. Consequently, New Year's Eve parties often include barbecues.

It is also very common to see fireworks in towns and cities across the country. Awards for good citizenship are given out in some cities. The awards are a way for people to recognize each other for being good neighbors and friends.

HAPPY
NEW
YEAR

Over 80,000 fireworks are set off
from Sydney Harbor Bridge and
other points around the harbor.

The word *Matariki* can mean "tiny eyes," and it refers to a cluster of stars that are visible after the full moon from mid to late June each year. The appearance of these stars also signals the beginning of the new year for the Maori people of New Zealand, as well as for other groups living on islands in the Pacific Ocean.

There are many stories about the significance of the stars. They are not only used for navigation through the waters of the Pacific, but also as a sign whether the harvest will be plentiful or not. If the stars are clear and bright, the year will be warm and productive. If the stars are hazy, or weak, a cold winter is in store.

The cluster of stars called Matariki is also known as the Pleiades.

Members of a Maori dance group perform for Matariki.

Matariki is celebrated at different times by different groups. Some people hold feasts when the stars are first seen. Others celebrate during the full moon, and others celebrate on the dawn of the new moon. No matter when it is celebrated, however, the appearance of the stars—clear and bright or weak and hazy—tells how Matariki will be celebrated.

During Matariki, the Maori and Pacific people educate themselves and others about their culture and past. They also learn about the earth and plant new trees to represent rebirth.

ARGENTINA   SWEETS FOR THE NEW YEAR

The name Argentina comes from the Latin word for silver, *argentums.* The native people gave gifts of silver to the first European arrivals around 1516. Today, Argentina is the second-largest country in South America, but it hosts a mostly European population; most citizens are descendents of immigrants from Spain, Italy, and other European nations.

In 2000, over 50,000 people attended the New Year's celebration in Ushuaia, Argentina.

The first day of the new year is often a hot one in Argentina because it falls during summer. Everyone is happy, however, because they are going to start another year.

Many people in Argentina celebrate New Year's Eve by having a big meal with their families. Two traditional foods are *turron*, a candy made with nuts, and *pan dulce*, or sweet bread. Another popular treat is *dulce de leche*, or caramel sauce.

People in Argentina also have special customs that they follow to bring luck in the new year. They wear new clothes, often pink. They also eat beans, which are supposed to bring luck. In addition, people will run around their homes carrying a suitcase so that they will travel a lot in the new year.

There are also parties in the towns and cities, where people watch fireworks. No matter if they are at home or in a town square, at the stroke of midnight, everyone cheers and wishes each other luck in the new year!

Turron, a candy made with nuts, is very popular in Argentina.

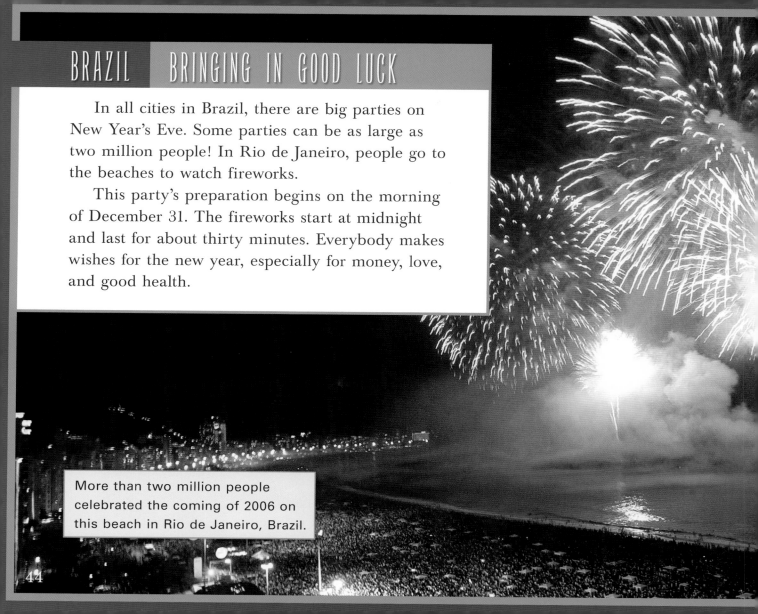

In all cities in Brazil, there are big parties on New Year's Eve. Some parties can be as large as two million people! In Rio de Janeiro, people go to the beaches to watch fireworks.

This party's preparation begins on the morning of December 31. The fireworks start at midnight and last for about thirty minutes. Everybody makes wishes for the new year, especially for money, love, and good health.

More than two million people celebrated the coming of 2006 on this beach in Rio de Janeiro, Brazil.

In Brazil, most New Year's Eve customs are supposed to bring good luck. Most people wear white clothes to bring them luck and peace in the new year. If people are at a beach after midnight on New Year's Eve, they will go in the water, jump seven waves, and throw flowers in the sea while making a wish. Some people also light candles in the sand on the beach.

In Brazil, the lentil, a type of bean, is believed to bring wealth. On New Year's Day, many Brazilians also eat lentil soup or lentils and rice. This custom, as well as many others, is thought to have come from the mix of the African and native South American cultures that developed in Brazil, and have spread from coast to coast.

People throw flowers into the ocean and jump the waves for good luck.

ten nine eight
seven six five
four three two one...

HAPPY NEW YEAR!

No matter where you celebrate or when, some things stay the same among all celebrations of the new year. People spend time with family and friends. They wish each other well, and they hope for the best in the next twelve months.

Next New Year's Eve, think about how many people are also watching fireworks and eating a delicious meal with their family. And give a cheer for a happy new year around the world!

Glossary

agriculture farming

crescent shaped like less than a half of a circle

cultural having to do with the way a group of people live

embers hot pieces of something burned in a fire

longitude imaginary lines running north to south on the globe

lunar having to do with the moon

meditation the act of sitting quietly and thinking deeply

resolutions promises

rituals ceremonies that happen the same way each time

shrines places where religious objects are kept

solar having to do with the sun

solstice the time when the sun is at its highest southern or northern point in the sky

Index